Simple

Richard Small

To Tony & Jane,
my good friends,
Richard.

Edward Gaskell
DEVON

Edward Gaskell publishers
Riverbank Cottages
Bideford
Devon
EX39 4AS

First published 2017

ISBN 978-1-906769-77-2

Simple Poems

Richard Small

Typeset, printed and bound by
Lazarus Press
6 Grenville Street
Bideford
Devon
EX39 3DX
www.lazaruspress.com

'We sit around in a ring and suppose,
But the secret sits in the middle and knows.'
Robert Frost.

Contents

Contents

By the same author

I Want to Tell You a Story
Ghosts and Things
Tales from Merlin's Pal

Dedicated to all those who may
not have listened in life but have
now made the effort to read.

Sharing

A swimming pool, four acre wood,
for his family – best he could.
Trees and swamps and two big lawns,
bats and buzzards, rabbits, fawns.

While over-ground the giant walked,
under-ground old Moley stalked
for worms on which his family fed,
then snug they went, to moley bed.

On his lawn he looked with pity,
for underneath lay Moley City.
Yet Moley loved those happy days,
building moley motorways.

On occasion, from his tower,
upon the mole hills he would glower.
Then one day he felt no tears,
both he and mole – were engineers !

So he and Jocey, Sam and Clare,
lived cheerful with old Moley there.
The woods, the air, it all did please,
both their loving fam-il-ies.

Our new car.

Brand new car, in pride of place,
happy smiles lit up the face.
Better than a trip to Paris,
God, they loved that pristine Yaris.

Two weeks pass with lovely motor,
all has changed for their Toyota.
While, on the phone, a re-spray sought,
they pray, one day, the culprit's caught.

**

Forgetful in old age.

His mind, on job, that must be done,
he climbed the stairs, his work begun.
Memory gone, to who knows where,
'What the hell's he doing there?'

He stared about and wracked his brain,
he thought and thought and thought again.
Back down the stairs, what else to do,
'Perhaps he'd gone, to use the loo?'

Standing baffled, in stair well,
by and by, he heard a bell.
'Meals on wheels? You're on my route.'
As bold he stood, in birthday suit!

The Walk is Over

All it needed was the Dales
to finish off my walking tales.
Having crossed them, I could boast,
that I had walked from coast to coast.

In the past I'd had some fears,
that's why it took me sixteen years.
To make it right and bring me smiles,
t'would only take me eighty miles.

To win such prize, four days I planned,
and off I went, with map in hand.
I did get lost – as others hinted,
path had changed since route first printed.

Committed now, to progress chained,
three flipping days it rained and rained.
When the storm ceased from the skies'
out came in force, the biting flies.

When weak on hills in hungry mood,
I dropped to village low, for food,
Soon stomach thought the throat was cut,
the only village shop, was shut.

When to Richmond town came me,
no room there was in B&B.
Though in the house, *'no room'* they said,
'You can use our garden shed'.

Grateful for their kindly thought,
and sleepless in a bed too short,
blistered feet were racked with pain,
while on tin roof it beat with rain.

Worst rain for nigh a hundred years,
felt glad sometimes, it hid my tears.
The mud, the pain, the sweat, the path,
God, I craved a nice warm bath.

At long last, to car returned,
my muscles ached, my feet they burned,
but after rest and after dinner,
this old man drove home, a winner.

Helvellyn Summit – also in the rain!

To Blighty Bound.

On my return, from Budapest,
my train stopped in Vienna.
If I now told you, all the rest,
I'd have to charge a tenner.

**

Old Moley boy, my friend.

Purchased I, a cliff top hut,
no guttering, no water butt.
A simple place, it has no frills,
with its purchase, moley hills.

To drive them from their moley camp
upon their spoil heaps I did stamp.
Such harsh action, I felt haunted.
old moley boy – was nothing daunted.

Through ground it is they nightly bore,
happy they, as hills grow more.
God knows, how many worms they've eaten,
in my hut, I know I'm beaten.

So now today I'll let them live
and from my plot some land do give.
Why do humans stoop so lowly,
so give a thought, for my mate Moley.

Keeping the way.

We all that walk this path shall find,
sharp thorns, that seek to tear and bind.
When darkness falls, the way seems long,
but trouble not, our minds are strong.
With hearts of oak and faith that's blind
we'll find at last, this path is kind.

Beach hut in winter

Faint breeze there was, through open door,
the incense smoke to waft,
one could not ask, for anymore,
as smoke, takes soul aloft.

In gloves with missing finger,
I wrote, to sound of sea,
seeking thoughts that linger,
to write, for you and me.

Sitting in that beach hut old,
I think it's time for home.
My hands and legs are getting cold,
my mind's begun to roam.

It's wood, and eight by ten, I'd say,
whatever that's in metric,
one reason why it's bloody cold,
it doesn't have electric.

Last laugh to the laughing seagull

Some silly singing seagull,
out upon my roof.
To drag me from my slumbers,
borders on uncouth.

I rise to listen more, but
it is a bit too late.
For me to hear its song again,
it wasn't going to wait.

Now I begin to wonder, as to
sleep, I cannot fall,
was that silly seagull singing
or never there at all.

Flight.

I'm loosed by man to travel free,
yet none alive, can hinder me,
and to a point, I'm highly strung,
e'en fore my journey was begun.
The deaf can try, with all their might,
they'll never hear my hum in flight,
and where I go, my feathers follow,
faster than the swift or swallow.
And when I land, it's gold I've struck,
though some would claim, 'that's archer's luck.'

**

Flight of the Great Goose

Kevin was the leader
great leader of the geese.
He had his missus with him,
she was called Denise.

Kevin said, 'it's getting cold,
it's time we're in the air.'
His missus said, 'I like it here.
this really isn't fair'

'Do as you're told,' he said,
'for I am *he,* in charge.'
She'd surely have to toe the line,
if she was not so large.

At last he had his way.
Denise agreed to go.
'Okay you bolshy gander,
I'll follow with the flow.'

High above the tundra snow,
Kevin was in heaven.
With eyelids shut, he dreamed away,
of a lake in Devon.

Didn't hear the warning shout,
he didn't feel a thing.
Now he's going home again,
upon a Jumbo's wing.

Denise, she could not tarry,
no wish to be kept late.
Now she'd lost her Kevin,
she'd find another mate.

The Missing

You might be dead,
or, so it seems,
but I still see you,
in my dreams.

**

A dream of times.

My mind is filled
with time gone by,
a place I never knew.
And visions open in my mind
of then, and me and you.

Of times gone by,
we may have known,
a truth within us wakes
and when we dream, how we were there,
to *there,* our souls it takes.

In harbours thronged,
our masted ships,
were readied for the sea.
Those left behind wrung hands with hope,
alone upon the quay.

As heroes sailed,
to far off lands,
many tears were shed,
for noble hearts they loved so much,
now, numbered in the dead.

Why should I care,
my mind to fill,
with heartfelt loss at sea.
Perhaps it is, that we've come back,
from then, yes, you and me

The Christmas Card.

Five days I watched the letter box,
and not a thing came though.
Then seventeen came all at once,
though sadly, none from you.

Such fears as come with policeman's knock,
not knowing, why or how,
and still I long to hear your news,
so missed in life, right now.

Bright envelopes of every size,
to open each, a thrill.
With eighty seven on display,
there's one, I wait for still.

**

Straw house – called 'huff and puff'.

Good friends of mine, they thought it fine,
to build a house of straw.
they even started up a blog,
so they could tell you more.

They stood in awe, as bits arrived,
made of wood were they,
and some they took four men to move,
backs bent into the fray.

The architect and planners too,
offered little aid.
vacant minds with little knowledge,
of even, how it's made.

At night, within their little house,
they worried in their beds
of cruck frames, falling through the roof,
to land upon their heads.

Tie beams were screwed, to flimsy rafters,
Lew said that they would win,
but holes he'd made to do the job,
just let the rain come in.

Though times it taxed, both mind and body,
when came the heavy stuff,
they'd lure a friend, down for a dinner,
he too, could huff and puff.

Blocks and battens, purlins, bales,
all secured with ties.
A green house look it had at last
and home for loads of flies.

But in the end, it will be done,
my friends, they will succeed.
Living in the house they built,
made of horsey feed.

No pigs nor wolves were hurt in the making of this poem.

Too often never sent, never read.

I'm getting old, I sense an end
and want to help, not to offend.
For bitterness and woeful strife
stand in the way to happy life.

If to the world, we kindness give,
a better way, we'll have to live.
Instead of hate, when heart does ache,
reach out your hand, for friendship's sake.

Destiny, or hand of fate,
it was your choice, if left too late.
Share some time, with someone dear,
before they are no longer here.

Were they honest, were they kind,
does a thank you come to mind?
If in life, this time you squander
for evermore, your soul will wonder.

Disturbing nature.

To nature's call,
they risk it all,
the Robin's eggs to hatch.
But in the garden death has come,
some bonehead's bought a cat.

Poem of dreams

As I drifted into sleep,
dreams came, I wished to keep.
Dreams opened up the doors for me,
I kept awake, that I could see.

Drifting into sleep, I saw
dreams that opened up more doors.
So that I, some notes could take,
I lay in bed and stayed awake.

Pen poised ready, with the book,
no doors there, for me to look.
Dreams, their secrets, they will keep,
as in a while, I was asleep.

**

The Railway Carriage.

Many years ago, the fire service took part in a multi agency exercise to test their abilities with a major incident. It involved railway carriages on disused track. The railway carriages were on loan from the train company.

It was in error, that they set,
the carriage well alight.
It burned so fierce, to their regret,
those officers so bright.

When we turned up, to put it out,
they, nowhere could be seen.
While borrowed carriage burned to nowt,
hid in their tents, they'd been.

'Not the smartest move', you'd say,
I wouldn't disagree.
Such skill is why they got high pay
and ordered you and me.

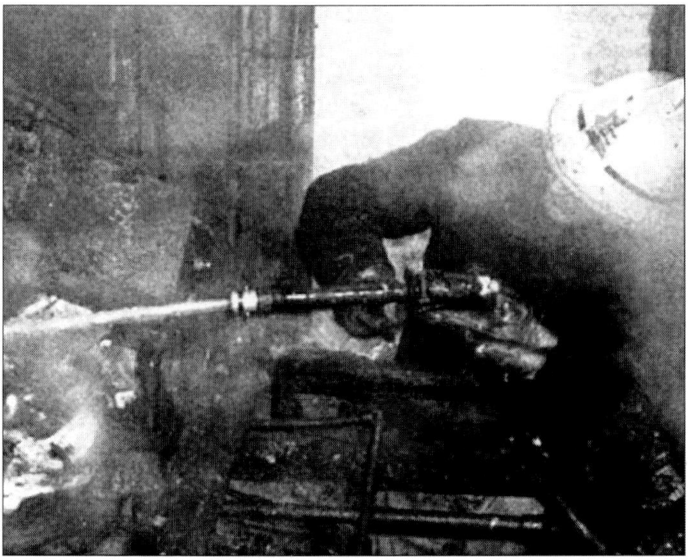

Author at the incident

photo by Nick Richardson

The love of life - Louisa.

(Inspired by the lifeboat, 'Louisa' of Lynmouth, in the late 19th century, when lifeboats were launched by man and horse and were rowed to the scene.)

Wild calls for help, bring with them fear;
maroons, they wake the night.
Calls, to men both brave and strong
and bound by hope, not fright.
The crew is picked, the orders clear,
the coxswain shares his plan.
She's launched into the pounding surf,
as only life boats can.

'Pull hard my crew,' the coxswain shouts,
'Pull hard for distant sail.
Through wind and wave and darkness,
I vow that we'll not fail.'
Back at the quay, the helpers stand.
When will the storm abate?
To welcome heroes home again,
their fearful hearts must wait.

Upon the ship the children cry,
the tattered sails cry too.
Their captain tired, he's given up,
not so, the lifeboat crew.
'Set off a flare,' the coxswain says;
'Twas done without a fuss.
As dark turned bright, the captain prayed,
'God's angels come for us.'

Then voices called from out the dark,
'You're saved, now come aboard,'
but robbed of prize and sacrifice,
the angry sea, it roared.
The ropes were thrown, and grapnel fast,
ship's timber it did grip.
With failing hands and racing hearts
they stumbled from their ship.

As one by one they made their way,
each felt the need to rush.
The sea, it wants to hurry too,
Louisa's hull to crush.
They sigh relief and comfort seek,
all huddled on the deck.
Now spirits high and bent to oars
they leave the sinking wreck.

Photograph from a painting by the brilliant
marine artist Mark Myers RMSA

Now turned for shore and distant lights,
oh, still so far from home
and homeward bound, they have to race,
white horses, and the foam.
The waves rise high and troughs sink deep,
the elements do rave,
determined not to let them go,
but put them in their grave.

That coxswain strong had other thoughts;
he'd seen it all before.
'Our good Louisa life boat,
will take us to the shore.'
While sound of surf at base of cliff,
bid the storm run free,
to know if they can make it home,
they pray; as so might we.

**

Every Village.

There's not a village in the land,
that did not volunteer,
the finest of their kith and kin
to risk both death and fear.

And soon it was, they landed there,
a place awash with blood.
A shock, no less they have to bare,
knee deep in stinking mud.

Not the same as they'd been told.
'You go, my boy – I would,
Yes, I'd go too, if I were young'.
How different, where *they* stood.

**

When danger came . . .

Not for them to say, 'We're brave',
though risk their lives they would,
when danger came with threat of death,
through hope and hell, they stood.
To a man, the foe they'd fight,
regardless of its form,
and danger comes with threat of death,
in darkness, fire and storm.

I know their thoughts; I feel their pain,
for with them, once I stood,
and danger came with threat of death,
but not once cry they would.
When fearful shouts for help came in,
loud bells would raise alarm,
then danger and its threat of death
was met with strength and calm.

The siren wailed, the road had cleared
and urgently they'd drive.
While danger stalks with threat of death.
'Hang on, 'till they arrive.'
That dreadful fire, it seemed to breathe,
and life to terror give,
as danger grew with threat of death,
they must not let it live.

Fire is dead and people saved,
the crew returned to base,
all danger quelled from threat of death,
relief on every face.
No coin they ask, but honour due;
reporters, beg their name,
though danger lurks with threat of death,
none who's there, seek fame.

National Fire
Training Centre,
oil fire.

Photo by
author

Tyne Cot, Ypres.

Photo by author,

Never to come home.

1917 France.

The call for help, was loud and clear,
I could not stand and look.
I joined a queue, that showed no fear,
to serve, an oath I took.

At training camp they fed us well,
though discipline was firm.
Our orders came - in line we fell,
'Tomorrow - it's our turn'.

Off to the front, we marched next day.
Arrived with blistered feet.
'Twas then that hell, it came our way,
the shrapnel, gas, the sleet.

Now even if you said I can,
I could not now, home go.
For t'would appear, that I had ran
in shame before the foe.

Our staunch resolve, it will not fold,
we've lifelong friendships built,
should I desert my comrades bold
I'd sicken with much guilt.

Upon a stone, let others know,
about, what we did give.
How from these trenches, we must go,
to die, so they shall live.

But now we stand, with guns in hand,
too late to make amends.
I'll find my peace in *no man's land,*
and lie beside my friends.

Cambrin Cemetery, battle of the Somme, France.

'I am well.'

(Winter, 1915, the Somme.)

In little cottage, warm and snug,
she reads his card again.
With trembling hands around hot mug,
she senses all his pain.

In bloodied, mud filled, foreign trench,
he writes her one last card,
and shudders in the cold and stench,
of freedom, won so hard.

In Every Place. . .

In every place, there was a face,
remembered with a tear.
And evil laughed, when sword it drew,
for those who lived in fear.

Their sons had gone, and answered call
to arms and fight the foe,
while back at home, far from the front,
how could their mothers know?

They only knew, when it was sent,
sad letter from the King.
Cheap telegram, it told of loss;
their son; it could not bring.

No place to grieve, their son, no grave,
such loss they could not hide.
They knew not how, or when, or why.
Damn that General's pride!

Long years they pass, and few are left,
lost souls, now carved in stone.
With poppies red, we still do mourn,
for nothing can atone.

**

The War to end all wars

(And for so many, it did just that.)

Are we as sad, as he once was,
to see his friends all killed,
to sing the hymns and utter prayers
as grave on grave was filled?

In trenches foreign, far from home,
he laboured night and day.
And with the gas came nightmares,
he prayed could go away.

So very rarely, leave it came,
for home, and part this strife,
to new mown hay and roses
and marry, his new wife.

By special licence they were wed,
dismay they yet must bear.
The telegram it said quite clear,
'Recall to duty, there.'

A farewell hug, a kiss goodbye,
so sad to go away.
But duty calls, to send our friend
once more into the fray.

Back, where blood of man and horse,
flowed red into the ground,
all through that mud they marched as one,
until their peace was found.

Voices in the grave yard.

Beneath the Yew and Holly tree,
I hear a voice that's calling me.
But wait; not true, they call for you.
It can't be me, for it is said,
for ninety years, I have been dead.

**

The day out visiting.

I thought I'd like to visit friends,
along the lanes and round the bends.
Though Sat Nav said, 'You'll do fine',
lots more cars, on road than mine.

A roundabout began the queue,
I joined the now, frustrated few,
praying that, with God's good grace,
between the cars, there'd be a space.

By two at least, I should arrive,
but at this speed, it could be five.
Oh to patience, glory be,
I got there just in time, for tea.

**

Brothers Souls.

Sons thought it right, to go and fight,
while mother knelt and prayed.
Despite her tears, and their brave hearts,
the Devil, must be paid.

The Souls family lost five
sons to the First World War

Advice for new students in Aikido.

If you are coming on our mat,
make sure that you, are not too fat,
and if you really want to win,
make sure that you, are not too thin.

If you want to learn to save,
when joining us, you need be brave.
But also useful, so I hear,
is, never lose, your sense of fear.

Always heed, the teacher wise,
But question what he does advise.
Practise well and peace you'll gain,
as long as you don't mind the pain.

Keen students fine, come through the door,
they love it all, they love the floor.
Once gi is bought with stroke of pen,
you won't be seeing them again.

On my advice, don't come to blows,
Aikido's secrets – no one knows.
Strength of gnat or strength of ox,
all Aikido - paradox.

**

In time, we understand.

What we did and where we went
who we knew and how time spent.
With youth's mind, we made our choices,
but age it is, that hears true voices.

**

The Cornish Archer.

Trevellyan was a yeoman free,
whose son was born to archer be.
To stand the ground and bend the bow,
for him, his father all did show.

The years passed by, till he was grown,
great archer he, the seed was sown.
And in the crowd, did such a feat,
as Cornwall's finest archers beat.

No stronger man, when in his prime,
did hunt King's deer, though it be crime.
To warnings dire he would not hark,
his every arrow hit the mark.

The story goes, ten strong it took,
when sheriff's men, the village shook.
They dragged away our hero sung
to gibbet grim, where he was hung.

Some say they see the archer still,
as twilight mists do hush the hill.
When noble stag does lift his head,
our yeoman's here, back from the dead.

**

Communication – name of the game.

Modern man with mobile phone,
more attached, than dog and bone.
Regardless if the call's a pest
to answer it, he cannot rest.

Staring at their mobile screen,
have no idea, where they have been.
Every text, essential knowing
but no idea, where they're going.

Coming home, all in a tizzy,
phone's been going - very busy.
Something's wrong, it drives her wild,
husband asks, 'Where *is* our child?'

Policeman stops them on their way.
'For use of phone, a fine, you pay'.
'But surely guv, it doesn't matter
if to my wife I like to natter.'

'No excuse,' the judge did say,
'For your sins, a price must pay,
I'll sentence harsh, you must not moan.'
As 'bing bong' went the judge's phone.

**

The Enchanting Guru.

Oh-Ummm and on, the chanting goes,
guided by, the one who knows.
Disbeliever shakes and giggles,
but even Gurus can feel niggles.
'Perhaps you'd like to share by half,
what it is, that makes you laugh.'
'Why, yes I will, indignant few,
what makes me laugh is watching you.
But what I find is more than funny,
how foolishly you part with money.'

**

Divorcee seeks new life.

Smartly dressed, he went a walking,
soon grins he saw, and people talking.
Safe home, all smiles, dream life begun,
unaware, his zip's undone.

**

The finest Inn you ever did see.

Tis said that in North Devon,
where moorland meets the sea,
there stands an ancient hostelry,
as friendly as can be.

With history old, and ghosts, I'm told,
and inglenook chimney
with landlord kind and bar maid too,
as pretty as can be.

To walk and rest or eat well,
then nothing can compare,
since at this place you're welcomed in
to finest dinner fair.

Local staff will make you smile,
the car park, it is free.
Ghosts, landlord, maid and inglenook,
no finer place to be.

If you would like to visit,
make haste and don't delay.
The Blue Ball Inn on Countisbury
will always make your day.

The Pub Ghost.

'What a night,' tired landlord said,
in the darkness, by his bed.
'Few others have such busy life,'
he mumbled, to his sleeping wife.

All was hushed and all was still,
at the inn, upon the hill.
Noise down below, he sensed a wrong,
as fire was stoked by someone strong.

As into darkness, he did stare,
He told himself, 'No one's there!'
For in the Inn, 'tween moor and sea,
every guest, in bed, they be.

Footfalls, on old stairs, came slow,
fear, within his soul, did grow.
Steady creaking of the floor,
God save him now, t'was at his door.

Door swung open, wife's voice said,
'The fire is banked, I've come to bed.'
So stood the one, he'd married fair,
But what is that? Still lying there !

Smoke

Silent, stealthy, slowly creeping,
Drifting, climbing, shrouds the sleeping,
Deadly, choking, slow now quick,
Its parent flames the stairway lick.
Searching, aimless, total now;
Smoke caresses the unconscious brow.

Uncaring, unknowing, slowly sinking,
Floating, leaving, has no inkling.
Without choice forced from its lair,
Life from its body goes, to where?

Searching, aimless, total now,
Tis not concerned to wonder how.
Is it really the end in sight,
Soul removed, no chance to fight.

Glimpsing, dreaming, spirit lacks,
strength to witness the fireman's axe.
Rescuers, quickly, in they break,
If only the victim could awake.

Written about 1979.

Blue Ball Inn, Countisbury, North Devon.

If you stand quiet. . .

North Devon sea mist slowly clears,
an Inn, your view, it fills,
just as it has, six hundred years,
on our, great Exmoor hills.

Gone, the crunch, of hooves on gravel,
no horses come this way.
But, in that mist, if softly travel,
past sounds, will bid you pray.

A curdled scream, the howl of hound,
as hunted, flee the chase,
heavy footfalls on the ground,
to Inn, with fear, you'll race.

Inside the Inn, it's very still,
Strange quiet, though you can hear,
Odin's army pit their skill,
'gainst Saxon sword and spear.

Eight hundred dead, or, so they tell,
spoke loud enough to catch,
how Saxon Earl did Ubba fell.
Quick, go and check the latch.

But time and tide won't wait for us,
a lifeboat trundles by.
Louisa's crew, they strain and cus,
yet, 'Onward!', hear their cry.

In storm they trudged, to Porlock Weir,
they've people there, to save.
And as they toiled, they felt no fear,
those men of old, so brave.

Young children's voices from the school,
Joyful they, and shrill.
Bell was tolled, grave deep, the rule,
in church, you'll find them still.

Dim candlelight – a judge, a court,
bowed starving, peasant stood.
Of poacher's kin, Judge gave no thought,
'For you, 'tis hangman's hood'.

As from this dream, you start to wake,
kind voice shows all is well.
'Tis landlord, who your arm does shake,
oh my, you've tales to tell.

Pub sign.

Dogs are welcome,
so are sheep.
The shepherd too,
the peace to keep.

**

Confused?

I search for some simplistic note,
confused by this and what I wrote.
It hardly seems worth half the bother,
now there's a thought, and here's another.

**

November day.

Yellow flowers, butterflies,
bumble bees and hoverflies
dancing, having fun.
Yet tricked by winter's Sun.

**

Winter Sun.

How odd, that winter sun shines warm.
And Jackdaw lands upon the lawn,
to feed on grapes I left for free,
cos they weren't good enough, for me.
Insects dance on air with glee,
outside the window pane, I see.
I have a thought that is quite numbing
- don't they know, that winter's coming.

**

John Bunyan –
'He, who would valiant be, 'gainst all disaster.'

Three years in Cromwell's army,
a soldier, John had been,
embroiled in death and killing,
when only just sixteen.

They bid him come and climb fine stairs,
his foot steps light and hale.
But Royalists all, had gathered there,
'Relent – or go to jail.'

Sad stairs did Bunyan, now tread down,
then to the prison gate.
He, in his cell, on Bedford Bridge,
still preached, accepting fate.

With scores to settle sat the judge,
year, sixteen sixty one.
Defying will of Charles the King,
John chose to stand not run.

Before you praise, please think again,
on Puritan cursed sin,
that made this stubborn soldier,
abandon wife and kin.

While in that jail, he stood his ground,
a time that could be halved,
twelve years outside the prison gate,
his wife and children starved.

Our Friend, Eric

In writing group, an empty chair,
invisible, the poet,
but Eric's spirit still sits there,
quiet, and all can know it.

In memory of Eric Smith whose kind nature and love of poetry inspired me to write my own.

Died 23rd June 2017 in Great Torrington

Lazarus Press